writing dialogue

A Book of Writing Prompts

the san francisco writers' grotto

authors of *642 Things to Write About*

foreword by Shanthi Sekaran

ABRAMS NOTERIE, NEW YORK

writing dialogue

I've spent far too much time watching and rewatching the scene in *The Godfather Part II* where Fredo Corleone sits in an armchair, trying to coax Michael to quickly wrap up an ill-advised deal. Michael knows that Fredo, his brother, is double-crossing him, but says nothing, gazing coolly down as Fredo grows at once more hyped and helpless:

> Fredo: "I'm your older brother, Mike, and I was stepped over!"
> Michael: "That's the way Pop wanted it."

Fredo pretty swiftly loses his nut, and a few minutes later, he's rowed out on a boat and shot.

What is it that makes this scene so iconic? Physically, not much happens. Michael stands and Fredo sits. The two brothers talk, Fredo frantic, Michael barely nudging past a whisper. The power of this scene lies in its dialogue, its verbal and physical expression, the positioning of the two brothers—all of which tell us everything we need to know about who's in charge, who will live, and who will die. When Francis Ford Coppola made this film, he had a script to work with, but he also had sunshine and shadow, vocal pitch, Al Pacino's cool seethe, and John Cazale's apoplectic temper.

Well, good for Coppola. But how do writers, with no camera at our disposal, use dialogue to create such nuance? How do you create a sense of dominance and submission without physically positioning your characters on a set? How do you capture backstory, volume, and tension without the tools of light and shade, sound and screen?

First, every writer must decide if the speech he or she seeks to put on the page is best summarized (e.g., He said he didn't want the milk, so I sighed and poured it down the drain) or presented in the classic opening-quote closing-quote fashion (e.g., "I don't want the stinkin' milk!" he shouted, to which I sighed and said, "Fine," mostly to myself, and dumped the stuff down the drain). When agonizing over which way to go, consider this: If your dialogue can reveal something of your character's personality, his way of carrying himself, or his investment in a moment, keep it, and do what you can to maximize its effect. If it's not performing one of these functions, go with summarized speech.

Once you've decided on dialogue, tune your ear and listen like crazy. What makes a distinctive voice? Vocabulary, accent, turns of phrase, pause fillers, verbal tics? Absolutely.

But true voice distinction lies more in attitude than in word choice or habits of speech. Does the character you are about to put in verbal motion walk into a crowded party and plunge into its center? Does she hover at the wall? Does she head to the kitchen and busy herself with hosting duties that aren't hers, just to have something to do? Your character's attitude toward this party will influence how she speaks. Maybe, fearful of awkward silences, she'll find the nearest guest and launch into a monologue, barely pausing to breathe, her speech a series of run-on, punctuation-starved sentences. Maybe she'll stand alone, be approached by a stranger, and answer in monosyllables and sentence fragments, afraid to fumble, unable to loosen up and speak freely. Maybe she'll ask and answer the usual introductory questions, her dialogue punctuated with body language that shows how bored she truly is with this small talk, party after party, the same music, the same crackers and hummus, the same questions and answers.

Dialogue and the voices that compose it don't exist in a vacuum, in other words. A character's attitude in a given situation—the stuff the woman above brought along to the party (bias, anger, fear, a half-empty flask of vodka, etc.)—informs word choice, sentence style, and how she treats the people she talks to.

Often, then, good dialogue relies on visual cues to inform its sound. Let's look at a passage from Annie Proulx's short story "Brokeback Mountain":

"Forest Service got designated campsites on the allotments. Them camps can be a couple a miles from where we pasture the sheep. Bad predator loss, nobody near lookin after em at night. What I want—camp tender in the main camp where the Forest Service says, but the *herder*"—pointing at Jack with a chop of his hand—"pitch a pup tent on the Q.T. with the sheep, out a sight, and he's goin a *sleep* there. Eat supper, breakfast in camp, but *sleep with the sheep*, hundred percent, *no fire*, don't leave *no sign*. Roll up that tent every mornin case Forest Service snoops around. Got the dogs, your .30-.30, sleep there. Last summer had goddam near twenty-five-percent loss. I don't want that again. *You*," he said to Ennis, taking in the ragged hair, the big nicked hands, the jeans torn, button-gaping shirt, "Fridays twelve noon be down at the bridge with your next-week list and mules."

Joe Aguirre, the farm manager, points "at Jack with a chop of his hand." That hand-chop does a couple of things. First, it gives the reader's eye something to look at. Without it, we'd be watching Joe, Ennis, and Jack standing in the farm office as lifeless as three old brooms. Second, the chop of the hand creates a visual slash that separates Ennis's duties (as camp tender) from Jack's (as shepherd). It's important that the reader understand what Jack's and Ennis's duties are, since they come into play later in the story. Readers could easily zone out during this relatively dry informational passage, but that single chop of the hand recaptures our attention. Joe's second visual cue, "taking in the ragged hair, the big nicked hands, the jeans torn, button-gaping shirt," gives readers a chance to look at Ennis, as someone would for the very first time. Moreover, it's a gaze that passes judgment. Note that the passage's two visual cues perform distinct functions. They're both doing necessary and unique work for the reader's eye.

Notice, also, the one instance when Proulx needs a dialogue tag, she goes with the simplest, most invisible option: "he said." That's important. For the most part, you want your tags to be purely informative cues to show who's speaking. If you go more complex than *he said* or *she said*, it should be to convey volume.

Compare:

"Give me back the book," he said.

To:

"Give me back the book," he hissed.

Or:

"Give me back the book," he whispered.

Unfortunately, most people can't help but go further, embellishing their dialogue tags with all kinds of unnecessary window dressing. Anyone who's opened a Harry Potter book knows how much J. K. Rowling loves her adverbs in dialogue tags. Here's a two-part exchange between Harry and Filch in *Harry Potter and the Chamber of Secrets*.

"Have you—did you read—?" he sputtered.
"No," Harry lied quickly.

I don't want to pick on Ms. Rowling . . . but let's pick on Ms. Rowling. Why must she use the word *quickly*? She wants her reader to know that Harry is speaking quickly, of course. But the way she's written it, the understanding will be intellectual. You want your reader to *viscerally*, not intellectually, feel the immediacy of that reply.

Here's the dialogue without the adverb:

"Have you—did you read—?" he sputtered.
"No," Harry lied.

The word *no* is a monosyllable. It's quick. It's abrupt. Like the lie. The tacked-on *quickly* is redundant.

Even better:

"Have you—did you read—?" he sputtered.
"No," he lied.

Replacing *Harry* with *he* speeds up the reply even more. The monosyllables create a quicker rhythm.

Finally, you could do away with Harry's dialogue tag altogether.

> "Have you—did you read—?" he sputtered.
> "No."

We know from context that Harry is lying. Why tell readers what they already know, especially if it slows down a supposedly quick reply? Also, notice the contrast between the two lines. Filch's is eight syllables long, made longer by em dashes, pausing, and sputtering. Harry's line is a single syllable. No tags in this final edit. No adverbs. The contrast between the two lines makes Harry's seem even shorter, the lie even more automatic.

The best rule I can think of for adverbs and other dialogue-tag embellishments is that the spirit of the addition (*happily, quickly, excitedly*, etc.) should exist *between* the quotes, not after them.

Compare this example:

> "I don't know where his shoes are," she said confusedly.

With this:

> "I don't—I don't know. Where are his shoes?" She trailed off, gazing around the room as if she'd forgotten where she was.

The second example uses sentence structure, interruption, and physical detail to convey the character's state of mind. Readers look at the second example and think, *She seems confused.* Dialogue is much more powerful when it leads readers to draw their own conclusions.

On a side note, notice the disjointedness of spoken language here. Good dialogue is often clunky, stuttering, incomplete. That's because our aim, as writers, is to make the speech as lifelike as possible, within the realm of literary possibility. (We're going more for an illusion of reality than pure reality. If we made dialogue completely realistic, it'd verge on incomprehensible. If you don't believe me, record your neighbors, parents, or siblings sometime when they aren't paying attention, play back the recording, and type it up, word for word. Prepare for insanity.)

I've mostly discussed dialogue as a one-man sprint in this essay, but good conversation has at least two sides, if not more, and I'd be remiss if I didn't close with a few thoughts about the brinkmanship that is great multivoice dialogue. Every action has its corresponding reaction, right? Dialogue, at its best, reveals how characters regard each other. This dynamic can be conveyed almost instantly, if done right. In *The Great Gatsby*, Fitzgerald manages in a few lines to establish the innate hostility between Tom Buchanan—Daisy's husband and Gatsby's rival—and Nick Carraway, Daisy's cousin and Gatsby's ally. Newly arrived from the Midwest, Nick visits Daisy and Tom, having not seen them for years. We start off with Daisy telling Nick about her child, and then move quickly to Tom and Nick:

> "She's asleep. She's three years old. Haven't you ever seen her?"
>
> "Never."

"Well, you ought to see her. She's—"

Tom Buchanan, who had been hovering restlessly about the room, stopped and rested his hand on my shoulder.

"What you doing, Nick?"

"I'm a bond man."

"Who with?"

I told him.

"Never heard of them," he remarked decisively.

This annoyed me.

"You will," I answered shortly. "You will if you stay in the East."

"Oh, I'll stay in the East, don't you worry," he said, glancing at Daisy and then back at me, as if he were alert for something more. "I'd be a God damned fool to live anywhere else."

In revealing character dynamics, Fitzgerald wields Tom Buchanan's dialogue in a few important ways. First, Tom interrupts Daisy as she's talking about their daughter. This implies an assumption of dominance, perhaps a degree of callousness. The hand he rests on Nick's shoulder could shade either fraternal or arrogant. Its shading becomes clearer with the subsequent lines. Tom's swift dismissal, "Never heard of them," shows how eager he is to diminish Nick. (I would argue that Fitzgerald could have done away with *decisively*. Tom's statement is decisive enough.) Nick gets testy and the tension becomes mutual. Tom replies with further derision: "I'd be a God damned fool to live anywhere else." Taking an indirect jab at Nick and Daisy's corner of the world, shooting the two of them that suspicious glance, Tom reveals a hostility that seems to brew in backstory; the reader can only hope its origins will come to light.

The possibilities for character dynamics are endless, but here are some I like to play with when crafting dialogue:

Admirer/admired. Whose gaze is focused on whom? Who hangs on whose every word? Is one person asking getting-to-know-you questions, while the other answers but does not reciprocate? Maybe the admiration is mutual. If so, the gaze, the listening, the questions might match.

Nurturer/nurtured. Whose dilemma is the conversation focused on? Who offers physical comfort—a hug, a hand on the shoulder? How are the bodies positioned? Is one body framed within another? Is one body protecting another in some way?

Dominant/submissive. Who talks more? Who interrupts or contradicts whom? Does one character seek permission or approval from another? Does one character stay calm, while the other gets frustrated? How are they positioned physically? Is one standing over the other? Is one fidgeting nervously?

Speaking of dominance and submission, let's return to the *Godfather* scene at the top of the essay. How would you dress up the Fredo–Michael Corleone exchange? Pretend you're writing for an audience that will never see the film.

Fredo: "I'm your older brother, Mike, and I was stepped over."

Michael: "That's the way Pop wanted it."

Fredo: "It ain't the way I wanted it! I can handle things. I'm smart! Not like everybody says . . . like dumb. I'm smart and I want respect!"

Michael: "Is there anything more you can tell me about this investigation? Anything more?"

Your job: Bring this dialogue to life (see prompt on page 16).

(see prompt on page 16)

. . . .

SHANTHI SEKARAN'S recent novel, *Lucky Boy* (Putnam/Penguin), was an NPR Best Book of 2017. The *New York Times* calls it "brilliantly agonizing." She teaches creative writing at Mills College in Oakland, California.

writing dialogue: a summary

- **Reveal more.** Dialogue should enhance the characters' personalities, how they carry themselves, their investment in a moment; otherwise, go with summarized speech.

- **Context matters.** A character's attitude in a scene, which might be conveyed through body language and interior monologue, is as important to dialogue as word choice or habits of speech. Your backstory influences how characters speak and informs their sentence style and how they interact with other characters.

- **Create movement.** Visual cues (gestures like a chop of a hand) create a more dynamic scene, giving the reader's eye something to follow.

- **Stay simple.** *He said* and *she said* dialogue tags should be used as needed to show who's speaking; adding embellishment like adverbs ("he lied quickly") rarely adds depth unless it's to show a change in volume ("he whispered").

- **Keep it real.** Aim to make speech as lifelike as possible on the page without it being incomprehensible. It should have the awkward, stuttering, incomplete nuances of reality while still being coherent.

writing prompts

power dynamics

Translate the *Godfather* dialogue between Fredo and Michael on pages 11–12 from script to prose, inserting character descriptions and body language to bring the dialogue to life.

_____

_____

_____

_____

_____

_____

_____

_____

_____

_____

_____

_____

_____

_____

_____

_____

_____

_____

attitude adjustment

Select a passage of dialogue and think about the attitude of one of the characters (how she views herself in relation to her situation). Now rewrite the passage and change the attitude of that speaker without rewriting the dialogue.

_____

_____

_____

_____

_____

_____

_____

_____

_____

_____

_____

_____

_____

_____

_____

_____

_____

_____

_____

_____

_____

_____

_____

_____

_____

_____

_____

_____

_____

_____

_____

_____

_____

_____

_____

catching tone

How might body language, facial expression, and attitude change the tone of your character's speech without changing the words between the quote marks? Think about introducing a note of sarcasm, ridicule, or hurt into a phrase where originally there was none.

bye-bye, adverbs

Manipulate the words and add visual, physical action to the following sentences, so they communicate the desired emotion without the adverb.

"Maybe we could go on a picnic," he said cheerfully.

_____

_____

_____

_____

_____

_____

_____

_____

"You can't mean that," she said desperately.

_____

_____

_____

_____

_____

_____

_____

"I have everything I need," he said emphatically.

_____

_____

_____

_____

_____

"How do you feel about meeting my parents?" she asked
uncertainly.

_____

_____

_____

_____

_____

"I'm going to tell Mom," she said savagely.

_____

_____

_____

_____

_____

_____

eavesdrop on a conversation

Record an overheard conversation and then write it
down, word for word. Observe how disjointed real-life
conversation can be.

_____

_____

_____

_____

_____

_____

_____

_____

_____

_____

_____

_____

_____

_____

_____

_____

_____

_____

_____

_____

Now try to write a scene using all or some of the dialogue you just transcribed. Complete it with visual and physical cues, and whatever description seems necessary.

_____

_____

_____

_____

_____

_____

_____

_____

_____

_____

_____

_____

_____

_____

_____

_____

_____

_____

_____

_____

_____

List all the alternative ways you can think of to say *she said* (she stuttered, she muttered, etc.). Remember: Use these only when you need to adjust the volume. Plain old *said* is best otherwise.

alternatives to *said*

_____   _____
_____   _____
_____   _____
_____   _____
_____   _____
_____   _____
_____   _____
_____   _____
_____   _____
_____   _____
_____   _____
_____   _____
_____   _____
_____   _____
_____   _____
_____   _____
_____   _____
_____   _____
_____   _____
_____   _____
_____   _____

add the action

Add dialogue tags and action to these quotes to reveal something about the character who is speaking (e.g., "I didn't do it" becomes, "Chris was shaking. 'I did . . . I didn't do it,' he sputtered.")

"I didn't do it." _____

_____

_____

_____

_____

"She's going to kill me." _____

_____

_____

_____

_____

"Why me?" _____

_____

_____

_____

_____

"I won." _____

_____

_____

_____

_____

_____

"Just wait. You'll see." _____

_____

_____

_____

_____

_____

"I'm fine. Really." _____

_____

_____

_____

_____

_____

_____

proxy for talk

Two people are unloading the dishwasher. Use their handling of the plates and silverware to nonverbally express their frustrations with each other.

_____

_____

_____

_____

_____

_____

_____

_____

_____

_____

_____

_____

_____

_____

_____

_____

_____

_____

_____

_____

alpha, beta

Write a dialogue between two people, one alpha (dominant) and one beta (submissive). How does each person react physically? Facially?

subvert expectations

How would this scene play out between the following characters?

- An administrative assistant (alpha) and his or her boss (beta)

- A high school student (alpha) and his or her principal (beta)

- An artist (alpha) and his or her wealthy patron (beta)

why today?

Two fishing buddies are out on a lake. Buddy A has been in love with Buddy B for years and finally wants to confess. Answer the following questions to develop the backstory for this scenario.

How and when did these two characters meet?

_____

_____

_____

_____

_____

_____

_____

Was A's attraction to B immediate or did it develop over time?

_____

_____

_____

_____

_____

_____

_____

How does B feel about A?

_____

_____

_____

_____

_____

_____

_____

_____

_____

Why has A chosen to confess to B on this day, of all days?
What is different about today?

_____

_____

_____

_____

_____

_____

_____

_____

drowning in truth

Back to the fishing buddies out on the lake from the previous page. Write the scene for A's confession to B, using pieces of their backstory to inform the dialogue.

_____

_____

_____

_____

_____

_____

_____

_____

_____

_____

_____

_____

_____

_____

_____

_____

_____

_____

_____

_____

Write a chain-link dialogue for two people. The rule here is that each time a speaker begins, they must start with the same word the other person ended with.

Example:
"Can I offer you some tea?"
"Tea would be lovely."
"Lovely seeing Alex yesterday."
(And so on.)

This isn't the sort of dialogue that will likely end up in a published piece, but it will help you develop your agility. Your goal is to write dialogue that pushes the story forward and doesn't allow the chain-link to stagnate it.

chain-link dialogue

_____

_____

_____

_____

_____

_____

_____

_____

_____

_____

_____

_____

_____

_____

_____

_____

_____

_____

_____

_____

_____

two languages

Write a dialogue in which only one person speaks; the other responds using strictly body language (gestures, actions, and facial expressions).

can't say no

For this dialogue, perhaps Person X proposes to Person Y; Y refuses the proposal without saying "no" in words.

dialogue or summary?

Put two people in a car they can't get out of. Let the scene
unfold using only dialogue. What do the two characters say
to each other?

_____

_____

_____

_____

_____

_____

_____

_____

_____

_____

_____

_____

_____

_____

_____

_____

_____

_____

_____

Using the same scenario, summarize what happens. (Which works better in this case, dialogue or summary?)

_____

_____

_____

_____

_____

_____

_____

_____

_____

_____

_____

_____

_____

_____

_____

_____

_____

_____

_____

escalation

A shy college student tries flirting at a bar. His confidence
builds with each beer. Show the escalation through dialogue.
Think about changes in tone, flow, and body language.

---

dinner is ruined

You've dropped a pot full of tonight's dinner on the floor, and everyone at the table reacts differently. Jot down the verbal reaction of each person present.

Your partner blows up at you.

_____

_____

_____

_____

_____

Your kid tries to make you laugh.

_____

_____

_____

_____

_____

Your grandparent reacts with zen cool.

_____

_____

_____

_____

_____

Your mother-in-law pretends it didn't happen.

_____

_____

_____

_____

_____

Your mother immediately offers a solution.

_____

_____

_____

_____

_____

You react badly.

_____

_____

_____

_____

_____

_____

_____

what happened before dinner?

Revisit the spilled-dinner scenario on the previous page. Write a multiperson dialogue in a way that weaves in subtle references to backstory to deepen your reader's understanding of what lies behind the characters' respective reactions.

_____

_____

_____

_____

_____

_____

_____

_____

_____

_____

_____

_____

_____

_____

_____

_____

_____

_____

_____

_____

power play

Write the dialogue for a job interview in which the interviewer has the power.

_____

_____

_____

_____

_____

_____

_____

_____

_____

_____

_____

_____

_____

_____

_____

_____

_____

_____

_____

Rewrite the interview so that the interviewee has the power.

_____

_____

_____

_____

_____

_____

_____

_____

_____

_____

_____

_____

_____

_____

_____

_____

_____

_____

_____

_____

_____

_____

....

Keep a list of verbal tics you hear out in the world. These go beyond *ums* and *ahs* to include transitional words, words and sounds tacked on to the ends of sentences, and sounds made to fill a silence. Create a dialogue between two characters who each resort regularly to one verbal tic. Use these verbal tics without overdoing them. Consider where you find yourself cutting them out or adding them in.

....

tic check

awkward and stuttering

A son sees his father for the first time in twenty years.
Relate the conversation with lots of hesitations and pauses.

_____

_____

_____

_____

_____

_____

_____

_____

_____

_____

_____

_____

_____

_____

_____

_____

_____

_____

_____

_____

_____

small, smaller, smallest talk

You know those people who just have to fill airtime with idle chatter, no matter how awkward? Create one of them on the page through dialogue.

confrontation

A woman suspects her husband of losing his job and not telling her. She confronts him in the car.

_____

_____

_____

_____

_____

_____

_____

_____

_____

_____

_____

_____

_____

_____

_____

_____

_____

_____

_____

Write the same scene with kids in the backseat.

_____

_____

_____

_____

_____

_____

_____

_____

_____

_____

_____

_____

_____

_____

_____

_____

_____

_____

_____

_____

_____

_____

make it believable

Write a natural-sounding dialogue in which you explain to your new partner that your mother is a mermaid.

_____

_____

_____

_____

_____

_____

_____

_____

_____

_____

_____

_____

_____

_____

_____

_____

_____

_____

_____

the first date

Write a dialogue in which two people on a first date are
mutually interested in each other.

_____

_____

_____

_____

_____

_____

_____

_____

_____

_____

_____

_____

_____

_____

_____

_____

_____

_____

_____

_____

Now write a dialogue in which one person is much more admiring than the other.

_____

_____

_____

_____

_____

_____

_____

_____

_____

_____

_____

_____

_____

_____

_____

_____

admirer/admired

If needed, refer back to the foreword to review the tools that help convey a dynamic of admirer/admired (page 11).

_____

_____

_____

nurturing negotiation

A mother knows about her teenager's breakup secondhand. She wants to broach the subject with her child without overstepping or causing embarrassment. How does the conversation go?

_____

_____

_____

_____

_____

_____

_____

_____

_____

_____

_____

_____

_____

_____

_____

_____

_____

_____

_____

_____

Try this same scenario with a father character and consider
what might change.

_____

_____

_____

_____

_____

_____

_____

_____

_____

_____

_____

_____

_____

_____

nuturer/nurtured

Again, refer back to the
foreword to review the
tools that help convey
a dynamic of nurturer/
nurtured (page 11).

the toast

You're at a dinner to celebrate someone who wronged you. You're asked to give an impromptu speech. What do you say? Your aim is to reveal how you feel about the person without stating it outright. Think about the subtext of the words you choose; maybe use phrases with double meanings.

_____

_____

_____

_____

_____

_____

_____

_____

_____

_____

_____

_____

_____

_____

_____

_____

_____

where's the car?

You're lying to your parents about the missing car.
They start off believing you, but then you give yourself away
somehow. . . .

_____

_____

_____

_____

_____

_____

_____

_____

_____

_____

_____

_____

_____

_____

_____

_____

_____

_____

_____

the mind isn't idle

As we lie, we think of ways to improve the lie, to make it seem like truth, and we wonder what will happen if we're found out. Try writing the dialogue with interior thoughts mixed in.

comfort levels

Six people have formed a book club. They haven't met previously and they're waiting for their mutual friend (the host) to join them. Write some dialogue for a group of people who barely know one another.

Fast-forward nine months. The same six people know one another much better. Friendships and factions have formed. How has the rhythm and volume of their conversation changed?

_____

_____

_____

_____

_____

_____

_____

_____

_____

_____

_____

_____

_____

_____

_____

_____

_____

_____

_____

_____

third wheel

Write a conversation between two high school classmates.
They have an adversarial and competitive relationship, and
one is trying to borrow the other's homework. After a few
lines, another student enters their conversation. How will the
first two treat the third?

_____

_____

_____

_____

_____

_____

_____

_____

_____

_____

_____

_____

_____

_____

_____

_____

_____

_____

_____

_____

_____

uses for a third wheel

Incorporate both spoken words and body language to explore any of these options for the newcomer:

- He or she is a welcome addition, but only from one character's point of view.

- He or she is an arbiter between the two adversaries.

- He or she behaves in a way that makes the adversaries band together.

elephant in the room

Two friends run into each other at the grocery store. Friend A just threw a giant barbecue but didn't invite Friend B. B knows about the party but tries not to let on. Write a dialogue that begins with B asking A, "How was your weekend?"

behind the scene

Before you begin, think about the backstory between A and B. Are they old friends or new? Do they like each other's partner? What sort of house does each live in? Why would A not invite B?

confession

"I'm pregnant," she said in a hushed voice. Finish the conversation. Use word choice and body language to reveal how each speaker feels about the other and about the pregnancy.

_____

_____

_____

_____

_____

_____

_____

_____

_____

_____

_____

_____

_____

_____

_____

_____

_____

_____

_____

you want to leave, don't you?

You need to get rid of someone who works for you, but you don't want to fire him. Persuade him to resign.

_____

_____

_____

_____

_____

_____

_____

_____

_____

_____

_____

_____

_____

_____

_____

_____

_____

_____

_____

_____

_____

inside, outside

One person in a duo does all the talking; the other person has a rich internal life but says nothing.

_____

_____

_____

_____

_____

_____

_____

_____

_____

_____

_____

_____

_____

_____

_____

_____

_____

_____

honesty, meet duplicity

Think of the possibilities. For example, one person says, "I need you to know I cheated on that test. You are the better student." The other person thinks, *I cheated, too, but I'm not gonna tell.*

fawning

Pick a famous figure you would like to meet. Write a dialogue in which this famous figure is generous and kind to you, even as you embarrass yourself with fawning comments.

Now write a dialogue in which the famous figure responds coolly to you, perhaps with annoyance.

_____

_____

_____

_____

_____

_____

_____

_____

_____

_____

_____

_____

_____

_____

_____

_____

_____

_____

_____

_____

_____

blame

After years of acrimony, Cinderella and Prince Charming decide to get a divorce. Write the dialogue for their final mudslinging argument.

liar, liar

Your friend is lying about his whereabouts. You listen for a while, then enter the conversation. Let's hear him, then you.

_____

_____

_____

_____

_____

_____

_____

_____

_____

_____

_____

_____

_____

_____

_____

_____

_____

_____

_____

_____

_____

things to consider

Is your friend lying about his whereabouts on a previous day? Or where he is right now? How are you hearing the conversation and entering into it? Why does your friend's dishonesty about his location matter to you? What's at stake for you?

inconsistent!

Show a character saying one thing and doing the opposite.

_____

_____

_____

_____

_____

_____

_____

_____

_____

_____

_____

_____

_____

_____

_____

_____

_____

_____

_____

_____

Show a character thinking one thing and saying the opposite.

_____

_____

_____

_____

_____

_____

_____

_____

_____

_____

_____

_____

_____

_____

_____

_____

_____

_____

_____

_____

_____

convert dialogue to summary

Using these lines of dialogue as a jumping-off point,
write a summary of what was done and said. (For example,
"I don't want the stinkin' milk!" could be converted to:
He said he didn't want the milk, so I sighed and poured it
down the drain.)

"You can't sit on me like that."

_____

_____

_____

_____

"Why'd you buy that?"

_____

_____

_____

_____

"I didn't want to say anything."

_____

_____

_____

_____

"I'm going to the store. . . . Be back in twenty minutes."

_____

_____

_____

_____

_____

_____

"I did my homework, and now I want to watch TV."

_____

_____

_____

_____

_____

_____

"Stop that right now and go to school."

_____

_____

_____

_____

crushed

You're having a party. On the way to the kitchen, you see someone you have a crush on sweeping up the shards of your favorite bowl. What do you say?

passive, then aggressive

A relative dies. The heirs gather. One of them is just out of prison for embezzlement. Read out the will and capture the dialogue of the family members.

_____

_____

_____

_____

_____

_____

_____

_____

_____

_____

_____

_____

_____

_____

_____

_____

_____

_____

_____

those kids

Record a few little kids speaking to one another. Transcribe the recording word for word.

Now make changes to smooth out the kids' dialogue but maintain its authenticity.

_____

_____

_____

_____

_____

_____

_____

_____

_____

_____

_____

_____

_____

_____

_____

_____

_____

_____

Designer: Debbie Berne
Project Managers: Meghan Ward and Danielle Svetcov
Art Director: Diane Shaw
Editor: Karrie Witkin
Production Manager: Rebecca Westall

ISBN: 978-1-4197-3831-9

Special thanks to: Alicia Tan, Alissa Greenberg, Ashley Albert, Audrey Ferber, Beth Winegarner, Bonnie Tsui, Bridget Quinn, Caroline Paul, Celeste Chan, Chris Colin, Christopher Cook, Constance Hale, Diana Kapp, Elizabeth Stark, Frances Stroh, Grace Prasad, Hunter Oatman-Stanford, Jane Ciabattari, Jaya Padmanabhan, Jenny Bitner, Jesus Sierra, Kathryn Ma, Kristen Cosby, Laura Fraser, Lindsey Crittenden, Lisa Gray, Lisa Hix, Lisa Lerner, Liza Boyd, Lyzette Wanzer, Mark Wallace, Mary Ladd, Maury Zeff, Maw Shein Win, Paul Drexler, Shanthi Sekaran, Stephanie Losee, Thaisa Frank, Todd Oppenheimer, Vanessa Hua, Yukari Kane, Zahra Noorbakhsh

Printed and bound in China

10 9 8 7 6 5 4 3 2 1

Abrams Noterie products are available at special discounts when purchased in quantity for premiums and promotions as well as fundraising or educational use. Special editions can also be created to specification. For details, contact specialsales@abramsbooks.com or the address below.

Abrams Noterie® is a registered trademark of Harry N. Abrams, Inc.

ABRAMS The Art of Books
195 Broadway, New York, NY 10007
abramsbooks.com

MIX
Paper from
responsible sources
FSC™ C144853